D1236164

Hilarity

Patty Seyburn

New Issues Poetry & Prose

A Green Rose Book

New Issues Poetry & Prose
The College of Arts and Sciences
Western Michigan University
Kalamazoo, Michigan 49008

First Edition, 2009.

ISBN-10   1-930974-83-3 (paperbound)
ISBN-13   978-1-930974-83-8 (paperbound)

Library of Congress Cataloging-in-Publication Data:
Seyburn, Patty
Hilarity/Patty Seyburn
Library of Congress Control Number: 2008938517

Editor   William Olsen
Managing Editor   Marianne Swierenga
Copy Editor   Kory Shrum
Designer   Abby Anderson
Art Director   Tricia Hennessy
Production Manager   Paul Sizer
                            The Design Center, Frostic School of Art
                            College of Fine Arts
                            Western Michigan University

Hilarity

Patty Seyburn

New Issues

WESTERN MICHIGAN UNIVERSITY

Also by Patty Seyburn

Mechanical Cluster
Diasporadic

In memory of Shirley Seyburn
In honor of Sydney and William Little

Contents

I.

A child of five would understand this. Send someone to fetch a child of five.

—Groucho Marx

When I'm not feeling so good

I go back to the dimestore of my youth
where they sell all forms of prophylactic against despair
and I sit at the fountain, on a vertiginous barstool
and pop the hectic red
balloon—it once contained the price of dessert
and a fortune.
Now it releases a Monarch, stained-glass
beating its way to heaven,
a map detailing a planet that could not resist
the sun's gravitational pull,
or a code of oval figures, whole and lonely
once the enemy moved to Albany.

I wander the aisles of ideology
while finishing a questionnaire
and I sample the rhetorical flourishes
with a lucid tongue.
My only answers are prime numbers,
because they are so clean.
Before I'm done my toes are filthy with falling
bodies, the detritus of dystopia—I can barely
scrape them off, I can barely prop them up
so I leave in a huff, arms laden with misfit
theories no one can stand, and I am
their viceroy, I am their Sandy Koufax,
I am their bag of chips.

I consult the bandaged palms,
their fronds behaving like odalisques.
Have they no shame?
An armada lines my street,
named for a fallen general in another war
between action and reaction.
Those soldiers felt pain in both shoulders,
which I diagnosed as a crisis of origin.
My history, too, has amnesia
and my cabinet members—or cabal, depending—

pressure me for my provenance.
Later, I say, we are later.
And: I have never been to Provence.

I read my teenage diary entries, and find
my pelf of wandering passions consumed
by the mealy bugs of time. I find I am
accomplished, my land fecund, my culture
advanced: my tourists perambulate flawlessly—
we have been working together each season,
so they understand the proper homage
paid each site: here's where I flocked,
I fled, defrocked, here's where I just
can't remember: all marked with plaques.
My natives reward their good behavior
with ritual facial ticks. We sell regret-
scented potions that go down like a bolus.

I freight a Shaker chair on my back up
Mount Blue, because there is nowhere to sit
in nature. One gets explanations only when sitting.
I fill my cheeks with water and practice
discrete swallows, as I am descended from camels.
It limits my conversation but all I know
is the chair, my life's work, having stolen each rib
from various Adams and whittled them to symmetry.
The legs are piney stumps of remorse
sacrificed for books' florid signatures.
It is worthwhile, even if they are pulp.
In the end, someone always carries me down
the mountain. Carry, oh
                    carry me down.

The Alphabetizer Speaks

I have my reasons

have never known starvation nor plenitude
and unless the order of the world
changes, I won't.
If the order of the world changes, I will
disappear, the way some vowels
elide into their word-bodies
or an individual blade recedes
into a field each season.

Will my daughter carry on this way?
I cannot yet tell her qualities—
if she prefers scale to chance, sequence to random.
And this may mean nothing.
I find chaos theory appealing, and eavesdrop on talk
of black holes, chasms, any abyss
that fetters sense. I relish
the desultory in many matters,
am slovenly, a slacker, a slave to caprice.
Except with the letters.

There is such thing as a calling
though I cannot speak for prophets or martyrs.
I have been summoned
by people of stature and the low-stationed,
comrade and debutante alike.
My eyes suffer, and my hands, my back.
I am my profession. It is no whim.
I do not want the world a certain way.
The world is that way, and I am a vehicle
on the road of nomenclature. I tend the road.

In my dream, all events coterminous—
no linear narrative, preceding or next.
The odd vignette, lone scene, an image
in isolation, no neighbors.
Then I awaken and pace

my thin balcony, calculating
how much of me waits above, how much
lives below, and I pose
the question of balance.

My name cues the turn home.

Where Were You, Nymphs?

Where were you, nymphs,
when I was learning to apply
the proper plaster of paris and papier maché
to fledgling cheekbones?
Where a nereid when I needed
advice on unguents?
A dryad to calm my riotous nerves
and dye my dulling locks?
An oread to teach the ablutions of adoration?
Sylph, you never paid the parson of insecurity—
where were you when these petty hips
toppled the girlhood world?

Put on your face, little goddess.
You'll need it.
Whittle yourself into shape
before Pygmalion gets here
and raises high the pedestal. He's not the kind we need.
No thanks to you, it all turned out quite well.
No more violin buying.
My cardsharping days are through.
I have exfoliated all layers of despair
and replaced them with voluble dew.
At this age, I rely on my looks, exclusively.
Don't think I'll send you my daughter.

The Myth of Rampion

For reasons, she
　　could not have
　　　　what she desired.
What to do?
　　Weep, wail, keen?
　　　　She could wallow
in despair. Swine
　　wallow with gusto,
　　　　glee. When Odysseus'
fellows were turned
　　into pigs by
　　　　that mean Circe,
their wants changed.
　　Circe loved Glaucus.
　　　　Glaucus loved Scylla.
Circe turned Scylla
　　into a monster
　　　　with six heads
and twelve feet
　　of dogs. (Poor
　　　　nymph. Lovely face.)
Whatever your story—
　　childless, craving, witch
　　　　for a neighbor—
wants are rampant,
　　greedy breeders choking
　　　　whatever strays onto
their acre. Fragrant,
　　they grow in
　　　　the garden like needs.

To Hope Street

Where I grew, roads named for their distance
from the river: 6 mile, 7 mile, 8 mile—
and the solemnity of numbers showed
resistance to artifice. Where I live

are neighborhoods of streets named for precious
gems—ruby, sapphire, pearl—and flowers—
poppy, camellia, lilac—displays plush enough
to harbor a felon, should the getaway car

expire. Here, even stucco buds—
tax dollars at play. Usually, it seems like Hope
wends places deloused of such luxury,
the drag from East Origin to West Destiny,

towns with city councils that meet in holy
donut shops. Here, west means you're going
toward the ocean and east means away, go back
from whence you came. I cannot go back

and neither can you. It does not exist—
those bustling Main Streets rusted over,
forlorn chassis in the Midwestern winter,
dead-ending into a field reclaimed by attitudes

of grass alongside a highway that pulled
a number so great it would surely be conscripted.
The dead and dying parade their nostalgia
down it wearing floats, risen above the fashioned

facts of memory. The street develops amnesia,
forgets its faults, dreams of asphalt patch.
Does lane aspire to avenue? Circle to thoroughfare?
I cannot help thinking that the street named Hope

has something to offer. Something prophetic?
Something narcotic? I cannot help
thinking, though I can't say it's time well-spent.
Ignominious hope, pedestrian hope,

a street is defined by its bounds: two sides
to every story. "Abandon all hope, ye who enter:"
the billboard outside Hell, according to the man
who layered Hell like a taco salad. If it will

make you feel better, you can cry
on the shoulder of the road.

Porcine Dilemmas

for Will

i.

Why must pigs stand in for us so often?
Consider the celebrated three *freres*
that went off to seek their fortunes,

their first impulse shelter. Their choice
of material reflects character, judgment.
Straw has that rustic appeal but gives in

too readily, and after such a blowing
down everyone carries the paladin dust
in their lungs and speaks in oom-las.

Sticks have a certain discretion and aesthetic
of the corporate, but cannot withstand
a singular gust. Clearly, brick's the best

choice, not facing but structural and
appropriately boiling water lying in wait
on the hearth was the last straw, as they

say, for the wolf whose aggression seems
unfounded. I miss the hearth—don't you?
Don't you miss gazing out at snowy banks

from the comfort of a heated interior?
It's a very French feeling, drizzled with
the buttery sauce of philosophy at twilight,

entre chien et loup though there is no dog
in sight, only the wolf of night in feral pose.
Myself, I miss nostalgia's spurious sighs

and cannot conjure its wide eyes no matter
how childhood blurs, how much and with
what furious speed I forget.

ii.

The complicated structures of language
demanding pig and toe conflate to perform
a range of metaphoric functions could only

have been developed by some repressed
linguist. The toes are pigs. The pigs are
people, they do what people do, in order:

go to market, stay home, eat roast beef,
have none and utter four immortal syllables
all the way home—one for each brother—

don't you think of them as brothers? Are all
pigs related? What could you and I possibly
have in common, beyond this nagging desire

for meaning, notion of too little time, craving
for intervention, divine or local? Myself, I think
the anchor drives the boat. I love staying home

and steeping my leaves in waters of
contentment until my brew is too strong
for those unpledged to me. We have all

had none of something, and such deprivation,
to a degree, softens the soul, though too much
makes one wander the aisles of anonymity,

file the forms of bitterness. As for
the repetition, who knows if the smallest
cries out in joy or pain as it rounds the corner,

if the newborn utters its first squeal in mourning
or praise? I like it out here just fine. These tunes,
human or porcine, are hard to tell apart, and

translation is an art that calls on talents
of origin, medium and destination.
Orwell knew this—who else speaks

so well for the pig? I can barely speak
for myself, as I gaze at the equality of
my toes and yours in wonder and wonder

at their docile pink cooperative.

There is No Escaping the Inedible

There will always be a dish
that can't be choked down:
the giant lima bean, or,
the slimiest of oysters.

Uruguayan mystics, the most
profound, say: each utterance
proffers purpose and accident.
So if a syllable or two

bellies up to the bar, boisterous
for shots of Patrón
and emerges in a blur,
forgetting its noun, all the better

to eat you with, my dear
says the tricky wolf of language:
what's meant to be
will happen, anyway, with/

out the crutch of cliché.

Pop Quiz

1)   Discuss the diminutive stature of the hero.
2)   Draw the face of futility.
3)   Debate: victim or predator?
4)   Can one emerge from the parlour, unscathed?
5)   Do the repetitions of "spout" and "rain" suggest:
         a)   the fluid, the arid?
         b)   the fecund, the barren?
6)   Write a dialogue between sun and rain where the sun explains ascent and the rain, her feelings of entrapment.
7)   The spider's action brackets:
         a)   the triumph of will
         b)   x as the inevitable.
8)   Demonstrate: ladder fingers.
9)   Wax poetic: "the sun's rounded arms."
10)   Filament, filament?
11)   Source? "Vertical, vertical . . . all is vertical."
12)   Why is the spider so often asked to stand in for *homo erectus?*
13)   Quest-romance? Bildungsroman?
14)   Down, down, down—*would the fall never come to an end?*
15)   Defend: the fly's vanity, her demise.
16   True or False: My Father's House Has Many Corners.

Cassandra in Surburbia: A Monologue

Two finches flew smack into my streaked kitchen window on the same day, and the fuchsia bougainvillea petals flung themselves in a torrid display shaped like Orion's belt. The peonies followed in the form of two dippers. I have ladles in both sizes.

My corn chowder refused to accept my roux. My blue corn muffins rose on the left, depressed and raw on the right.

The school board vote was held on 2-02-02, and they fired a teacher of mathematics whose first name was "Anna" or Hannah" for her daring décolletage.

The bathroom faucet drips in a coded manner, and slightly stains the porcelain with a carmine mineral. Its incessance reminds me of childhood.

My lime Jell-O containing cream cheese and mandarin oranges in the Bundt mold emanates like a crop circle: it attracts and repulses. I cannot slice it for fear of repercussions.

When I cut the crusts from tuna fish sandwiches, the pieces render the deuce of spades.

When I went to throw salt over my shoulder the shaker was vacant; only rice remained, dutifully absorbing moisture.

At a recent block party no one used words beginning with "g" all afternoon, and flags were sullen, though my German potato salad was a hit.

Our local topiary have become animated in conversation.

I know you won't believe me—don't you think I'm used to that? On Thursdays, Tiresius and the Cumaen Sibyl come over for Bunco and Cribbage. He spills, she twitters. We play for pennies. The occasional future.

We rarely roll the die.

B'rachot: A Catalog

for Sydney

One for grass (field of sighs).
One, perfect pitch (voice's veil).
Clocks (sun's ascent, demise)—
you name it: blessed, wholesale.

One for bringing me to this day
should not be repeated for the same
event but once in thirty days—
attrition by repetition

when I always thought
the strategy of prayer, accretion.
Since you cannot form the sounds
for the soul's return to the body,

I will—including your thanks
for middle and index fingers,
which sate you until the hunger says,
cry out, in perfect pitch—innate to infants.
All: *cry out*. (How loud the finches!
A regular Friar's Club meeting. A ten-hen party.)

I have told you that birds say "chirp" and "tweet"—
please understand, I am a poor translator,
living off one flat ear while the other
berates the past in triple-meter,

counterpoint of Cossacks on horseback,
fields of conscience underfoot.
I am incapable even of mimicking
you mimicking me,

and so we wait for the lift
in Babel's lobby: our speech will never
grow less confounded
than on this day—*yom zeh*—today,
to which we have been brought.
The why I do not know.

Once More on Free Will

Whether the painted lady needs to fly
to fulfill its mandate or, waiting for
clement weather,
will die in our toystore
habitat, my daughter performs

the best sort of interpretive dance,
the unconscious, unselfconscious kind,
mimicking our guest's
fits and starts as it finds
her wrist then darts toward

the ivy where it spies another of its ilk,
another home-grown survivor
and since its brain
cannot store ire
or gratitude, since the word

flutter moves in odd geometries about us,
we witness the folding body's translation
of the movement from
fettered to un-,
begetting that twist in the gut we recognize

not as the mourning of chosen limits
but straight-up envy. Are we better off?
My girl cuts and paints
a rose petal
with sugar-water, choosing

attachment and the inevitable treason
of flight. The creature leaves us
for leaves unknown and
my daughter cries—
cold comfort, the gift of reason.

Corot's "Girl in Pink"

Rendered with affection, a lover's line,
we're told she was a peasant girl who posed
for him, a passing pastoral whim, defined
by costume—pink skirt, white blouse chosen
to reveal an arc, a crest of creamy skin.
The object-of deserves our petty ration
of imagination—unceasing, restless din—
so goes it with creation.

An image strikes. No reason is apparent.
From light and pigment, flesh. From nothing, all.
This is no brush with art. Return her stare—
you see, you have been seen—the Arranger
of Perception, the "Infinite I AM" has called.
Call her what you will. Your life will change.

Instructions for the Good Life

Dust off your car's bloated user's manual
    the classics you've lied and conversed about
    —*Middlemarch, Clarissa*—
    hymnals that advocate the household gods and choreography
    of legend.
Study a dead tongue.
Speak in a rhythmic translation.

Watch chronological Truffault
    John Ford
    all the old Prisoners in sequence
    elementary claymation
    shows that trigger the impulse to purchase—it only takes a minute.
Buy a spinet.

Hire a tuner named Wardell whose father is a tuner
    brother is a tuner
    son is—yes, a tuner.
Practice minor seventh chords
    diminished
    augmented
that do not resolve.
Do not absolve anyone.

Register for correspondence art class
    divinity school.
Show up every day.
Draft 316 laws about the end of days.
Act as though Nothing could Happen.
Resign your post as
    the yeomen of wholeness
    the keeper of fraction.

Plot your happiness on a graph with X and Y axes—the result should look
    like a cat named Geoff.
Favor plot over character.
Borrow boring porn from an anonymous neighbor
    a numinous neighbor
    a third cousin whom you, technically, could marry.
Admire the sine wave's sinew.
Crave the lineaments of gratified desire.

Quote: "A dream is one-sixtieth of prophecy."
Wear a sarong
          a monocle.
Learn Pinochle
          Mah-Jong.
Draw stick figures in the dusting of coke in your old boyfriend's
          peppermint box.
Quote: "A man who goes seven days without a dream is called evil."

Memorize the names of Greek columns.
Campaign against the conventions of beauty.
Feign an affection for truth.
Invent the 20th century.
Turn to salt.
Salt to taste.

II.

Brooding, she changed the pool into the sea, and made the minnows into sharks and whales, and cast vast clouds over this tiny world by holding her hand against the sun, and so brought darkness and desolation, like God himself, to millions of ignorant and innocent creatures, and then took her hand away suddenly and let the sun stream down.

—Virginia Woolf, *To The Lighthouse*

What I Disliked about the Pleistocene Era

The pastries were awfully dry.
An absence of hummingbirds—
of any humming, and birds' lead
feathers made it difficult to fly.

Clouds had not yet learned
to clot, billow, represent.
Stars unshot, anonymous.
Moon and sun indifferent.

No one owned a house, a pond,
a rock on which to rest your head.
No arc, no here then there. Beginning
meant alive. The end was dead.

Art still a ways away—no lyre.
Beauty, an accident. Needs
and wants bundled like twigs
then set on fire. Except, no fire.

Candles had no wicks. Fruit
lacked seed. Books bereft of plot.
Ornament and condiment
were empty cisterns. There *were* pots.

It was pure act. No motivation,
consequence, imagination.
Sometimes, a flare, a glow, a gleam.
No questions asked. No revelation.

And I was not yet capital I.
Still just an eye. No mouth,
no verb, no AM to carry dark
from day, dirt or sea from sky—

God not God until one dove
called out "where the hell's dry land?"
An answer formed. A raven shrugged
and toed a line across the sand.

New, the sand. New, the vast
notion of this long division.
New, the understanding that
this time, there would be no revision.

In re:

Duck! God!
—Jack McKasson

the ocean

You must admit, it was inspired.
        At first, I thought the waves
should go out, originating
        at some juncture in the sand.
I considered lifting them up,
        completely vertical. (Someone
had the gall to call that "heretical.")
        Finally, I arrived at their present state—
in constant arrival, in tiers, a series
        hemmed by white spume, whitecaps—
a little ornament, like the eye on
        the peacock's wing. I have an affection
for frills. Some say they're all that—
        eyebrows, cheekbones, attractive
curvature, ligature. What's so
        wrong with detail? At first, the sea
had no "qualities," no physics
        and my archangels complained.
I granted sound to Gabriel, taxed
        by the scales of justice; smell to Michael,
wearied by cutting people slack
        "all day, every day, with no reprieve;"
taste to Raphael, who claimed
        healing futile; and texture
to Uriel, who rued illumination
        as too metaphorical—"not that I
can't handle it," he said. Then I
        stood back—one must delegate.
Our only debate over taste, as I
        resisted salt. Consider cinnamon
or ginger, I said. What soothes
        can also be bitter, said my angel.
I toyed with sky down, water up,
        but in chorale they protested

on logistical grounds. As for depth,
        I took suggestions and decided
"beyond what they can fathom."
        I'm loathe to tell whose idea that was.
Let's just say, he no longer works here.

the balcony

Get a load of that view.
There's Catalina Island—overpriced
but worth it, a pledge of paradise
coarsened, slightly, by the bicycle for rent.
I can measure the length of the San Clemente pier
from here.
How it bullies my water,
gesturing to the waves: go around!
There's always someone like that, pounding
the gavel of self-interest—if I punished
them all, there would be no time for diversions
such as this moment, an immersion
in lavender, which is not obsequious.
The irony: these interruptions, their constructions, contribute
to the panorama—a tribute
to horizon. How fortunate they realized perspective!
They surprise me
(particularly, their eyes).

umbrellas

I take full credit,
even for the truant ones
strewn on streets after a storm—
such triage.
And those chaperoned by wind,
beckoned up, up, up
their owners' hands abandoned,
palms in supplication.
I am infatuated with them.

So they didn't rate the first seven days—
I knew someone would
dream them up.
Look at my palms, their fronds, their lines.
Don't tell me Louie Parapluie never saw a palm—
one only needs so much imagination
what with allusion
and translation.
Do I need to draw you a map?

My favorites have handles like scepters
and abundant domes.

sand

It's not mine
but I should have seen it coming—
the gradual pulverizing—you know,
eventually it will all disappear,
as will you.
I did not mean for everything
to get smaller.
I did not mean for the rich, richer
and the poor, poorer,
nor for everything to be fair
though my translators
bandy about "justice" and "righteousness"
with abandon
as though words were meant to correlate to thoughts.
As though ideas matter.
And things matter.
Do dunes compensate?
I did not invent intent.
You did.
And the way indented footprints disappear
on the ocean's arrival?
That was yours, too.
How eloquent.

Your Name in the Title

When you are tired of defending
  your truths and ruses,
    come talk to me.
We'll choose the two foods we'd eat
      daily if we were dybbuks
        invading strangers' bodies
or archangels whose residue streaks our windows
      after the rain—that is their
        system of symbols.

When tired of stroking the murals of blame,
  come talk to me.
    We'll watch the surfers
slide a fiberglass chance across waves' sill—
     they fail and venture out again—
no victor or vanquished, no *mea culpa,*
      no roulette of contrition
      and forgiveness.

Here, guilt is tossed around like a basketball
  no one handles for long.
    And if you believe such
dispensation makes one shallow, so it does.
     Docked in the deceptive
      San Diego creekbed,
a dredge trolls for silt, and gnat-catchers
     that fled the fiery hills
      are back in time for lunch.

Don't turn off Coast Highway to head inland—
  it's no safer there.
    Don't turn off the radio
while it's playing that song with your name
    in the title
     that made you briefly
famous through no action of your own.
     Don't burn notes
      in hand-held fires,
watching words crackle and blacken.
   Haven't you atoned
    enough for one day?

Let someone else confess. The humidity of history
keeps the past fecund
for revision. And when
it gets too hot, the marine layer screens us
from bullying light,
the angel of blame.

First Bookshelf

There is a duck lost at sea when
his crate breaks after the boat is
destroyed. Tossed, overturned,
claimed and buoyed by a frigid
ocean, he observes the moon and
stars, knows loneliness, isolation
and lack of purpose. He wonders
if he'll find a home. There is a
monkey who makes countless,
thoughtless errors and manages
to redeem himself with friendly,
anonymous counsel. He makes
great messes and never seems
to gain an awareness of what
others endure on his behalf. He
is not held accountable for his
mistakes. A royal elephant has
appropriate adventures and an
extended family. A huge dog
with morals means well but his
size often inhibits his ability to
reach his goals. He frequently
learns to compensate for his errs
by giving rides, providing shelter,
protecting the meek. There is a
mouse with balletic grace, while
her tiny cousin has nothing but luck
and the charm of the weak: you
can't choose your family. There is
another mouse, crudely drawn in
primary colors, whose exploits are,
at best, prosaic. She keeps company
with an elephant, an alligator, and
a female of ambiguous species.
She drives a bus, cleans house,
bakes gingerbread, takes a bath,

attends the fair. She is middle class.
And yet another mouse, with many
paid friends and a girlfriend, sister
or cousin, also paid. They used to
keep silent but have, of late, learned
language, which has increased their
popularity but drained the pathos
from their exploits. A company of
pigs, an obdurate spider, a ravenous
caterpillar that endures change and
sheep: lost, defiant, naked. The duck
story is somewhat true except that
we are given the duck's perspective,
which must be questioned, as we have
no small stake in believing that we
are the only ones who understand
that we exist, with little notion of why.

Break, Break, Break

The daughter is louder than the sea
when the waves are calm
and she is not.

When the tide meets her on shore
she greets it by fleeing
into the blur

of a hot sun's circle and a degree
of sprawling cloud.
I watch,

not from afar. The waves
crawl up my thighs,
my arms,

recede, and otherwise, ignore me.
I warn them: *do her*
no harm.

A set conveys my empty threat
out to the powers that be.
They ripple.

If waves can laugh, this is a funny day.
Say what you will,
they say.

Anatomy of Disorder

I know that longing
listens to the surf report:
("Don't bother. No waves. Hope on the Northwest horizon")

and burrows its head
in Psyche's sand, emerging
a castle with turrets, drawbridge and moat, subject to fits

of mutability. Capability Brown
reshaped the English Garden
from contrivance to the articulated wild. In his perfect hermitage,

he was heard chiding a child:
"You can't escape landscape,"
and there you are on the back road to beauty and the sublime,

where the service is terrible—
they have no work ethic,
those two, always *Me Me Me*. We say: pipe down, you're nothing

special, but they keep
emerging—bedraggled,
buoyant with threat and decree. When Virginia Woolf put stones

like literature
in her pockets
to weigh down her corpus, and took a constitutional into the waves

that broke and broke
and broke, each stone
had its own shape, its own responsibility—complicit, along with the sea.

III.

It was said in the name of Rabbi Bena'ah: "There were 24 dream interpreters in Jerusalem. Once I had a dream and consulted with every one of them. This one interpreted for me one thing, and that one another. And they all came true."

—Babylonian Talmud, Berakhot 55B

All the things one has forgotten scream for help in dreams.

—Elias Canetti

Psalm to Night

I loathe the clutter of day,
                    competition of image and voice.
It has a short temper, short memory.
The work of memory;
                    the work of fiction.

Some claim you inscrutable,
                    remark on your opacity.
I say, choose: prophecy or recipe?
I reason better during your term,
                    the filaments of law extinguished.

Then can I ransom my shards,
                    retrieve them from righteous disarray.
Then can I free my doors
from the tyranny of welcoming,
                    my windows from explicit behaviors.

Who is like you,
                    oh hours of repute?
Who is like you, oh inconsolable?
When else can imagination and the chill wind
                    meet to cast the key of rain?

You are not the Angel of Death's quarters,
                    no railroad flat for the fallen.
Your purported silence, mere fable.
I find more absence at noon,
                    more vacancy at day's nadir.

There are those who malign you,
                    who would cast you out,
who consign you to the trope
of the lonesome, the claims
                    of solitary angels—

they are not so holy.
       I have bested them in dreams.
I have met them at dawn
and extracted the blessing of dew
     and my daughter's first cry out:
                an embrace of you. A denial.

I, Your Soul,

nightly sequestered from your body—
      restless peignoir, kid glove—retire
to the Liquid Lounge off the freeway
      in Garden Grove, guarded by
a flaming sword that turns every way and
      the cherubim bouncers know me by
no name. They serve dark beers and brats—
      cash and carry—though in my line
we don't suffer coin or pockets that
      carry the detritus of commerce,
longing to be filled halfway to express
      their state of discontent. A stop at
the small hangars to polish the wings of
      prop-planes—I try to leave a residue
of caution to counter the hubris of
      dilettantes. I visit your mother,
whose soul prefers to sit on the black
      leather couch next to where she dreams
of remembering and chases an elusive
      image into corners where her long-gone
mother surely sweeps the vocatives
      of Pinsk into Jersey City vowels.
I like to test the spider-webs to measure
      tensile-strength and when the weave resists
acting as sieve, I struggle with pleasure:
      no filament has trapped me, yet, though
I am hopeful—that would be a true
      consummation. Once, I lived inside
a carmine maple leaf and relinquished
      my hold when gravity beckoned.
Once, inside a Bird of Paradise outside
      Ralph's, vain ornament attended by
a hummingbird, wanting for nothing.
      So go my bachelor nights. I end up at
the drycleaners, submitting to the steam
      and press—light starch—so I can return
at dawn unsmudged, full of anthem
      and paean, and you, burdened by clay
dimension and the penalty of
      blood, do not feel the great weight of me.

Twelve Twelve A.M.

Who carved that frieze? Tinted that fresco?
Imported that marble from the toe of Italy?
The architecture of darkness turns
furniture to monument.
(Galatea chose the reverse commute.)

A bloom suggests; a tomb decrees.
No wonder the dresser drawers
stick, clad in shadow.
Bask in it. (How *unheimlich*!)

I wish—I wish—I do not know what to wish for—
just another night in the conditional.
Swig from a flask of sighs.
A river, a bird, a pot, a well.
The subconscious—such a peacemaker.

A dream of broken eggs means my petition granted.
This holds true also of nuts, cucumbers, all
vessels and glass and
breakable things.

One-Oh-One A.M.

Shards of a symphony imposed
on the pentimento of an electric guitar arguing
pitch with a piccolo: the orchestration of night.
It takes great talent, what with all the divas.

Cue the crickets. Cue the junebugs.
Cue the sliver of a moon.
Enter Venus and Sirius, downstage right.
Enter a ghostly disposition, stage left.

Ah, the overture: a piece with many codas.
Don't fret, little one—
the rectitude of an upright bass
is not in question.

In the instrumentation of dream are many trombones,
the slide and slippage of image
and due to their deceptive clarity of tone,
all too few flutes.

At this hour, everyone's an alto.
And the stars, as usual, are so hungry
that they pillage the veranda,
feral and vocal.

One Twenty-One A.M.

Full moon through clerestory slats.
Pursuant mist.
The room persuades me of
the logic of inanimacy.
The mirror's mereness in the body
of so much evidence.
How is it that so much comes clear at this time?
How are you faring in the whale's belly of sleep?
My belly is alert to possibility, an ululant sea.
It's a gothic night—you know the type—
all shroud
all supernal intimations of beyond.
Anachronism crowds the house's portals.
My turn, my turn, it says.
This is a deciduous world,
full of falling offs.

Two Nineteen A.M.

In dream you attend
the high church of disbelief
and tongue the tongue of a great bell
that volleys your name, your name
so there are two of you.

Gone, dream. Gone, vision.
This rocking chair is just right.
That bed looks good.
You wouldn't mind some porridge.
There are three of us, too.

Imagine a ring around her head: gold, white, yellow.
History told in haloes: explicit, invisible, aglow.
The more you say halo,
the more you think halo,
the more you feel like someone else—

hey! Is this transcendence?

Three Thirty-Nine A.M.

How impossible to be where one is
when the spider plans
its insurrection.
Your fingers qualify your thighs
and shadows secure their positions.
Even the mirror
having no need of reflection, gives utility
a holiday.
And still, though still, or somewhat, you are only half
there, unshelved, yet not free.
Empathy drains from the sieve of days,
threatening to rend us
even more remote from
the suffering we have been spared,
the joys we once translated.
The craving to hear another
say, "YES, EXACTLY"
enlists all your organs in its petition—
signatures amass, petals flung at a wedding.

Still Life on Holiday with Nightmare

Oh, hello

mortality. I am surprised
at your account, your earnest symbols—
I've never performed the sport you chose as my demise:
too many props, opportunities
for failure in Technicolor proportion—
no nuanced grey for these woeful omens.
Bits of bright shroud still cling to my digits.

Though on foot, I was vaguely vehicular
and my arms were full of broken things
I tried in vain to fix. And with life itself
sleeping in the next room, beneath a diaphanous
drape of pulse and rain!

Soon we will be home on familiar terrain,
and you know which drawer contains
the bevy of terrors, so why not repair
to a nearby spa until your posse of shadows regroups?
At seven A.M. the first airplanes rise

steeply before arcing East, home to the wells
of reconciliation—Rebecca drew clear water
for Isaac's manservant, her first scene in the recitative
of faith. Where is the Redeemer of Dream?
West, we dare to live at the edge

of the planet—don't believe that Galileo,
he looked poorly in short pants, fashion his foe
in matters sartorial and scientific. To be of one's time
is a curse! Better to rebel. I awoke when
my missive from the abyss
was returned for lack of postage. When I awoke
no flower of paradise lodged in my fist

as a record of my journey.

Insomnia Manual

Interrogate the origami light on the ceiling.
Amend your heartbeat to the fan's percussive hum.
Glance at the empty glass within arm's reach.
Wonder if hopes are barnacles.
Ask if expectations must be shed to lead a life without perfidy.

  Make a list of synonyms for "zenith" and "acme."
  Alphabetize them in lieu of a sedative.
  Lay your hand on your lover's hair as though conferring a blessing
    and wonder if it enters his dream.
  Wonder if it's rude to barge your way into a dream.

Speculate: your soul yearned to return to your body and couldn't wait
    until the alarm's coarse interruption or dawn.
Speculate: you ate too *nouvelle* at dinner.
Stretch, felinely—you don't give a damn about others.
Yawn.

  Recall the tidal sirens traversing the streets of your youth.
  Picture your father reading from a book of rhyme.
  Remember the terms of your truce with the attic ghosts.
  Consider religion's rationale for death.
  Wonder how the holy sleep at night.

Bring the room's inanimates to life; slay them.
Hope that your daughter finds imagination, reason.
Hope that she has your hands, your lover's feet.
Listen: Jeff the fireman leaves for his shift.
Listen: Barky the Dog salutes him.

  Create an isthmus of light between the two largest stars inside
    your eyelids.
  Return them to their archipelagic state.
  Think about blind Milton, "When I consider how my light
    is spent . . .".
  Think about deaf Beethoven unable to hear the applause.

Imagine: this is your real life.
Imagine: this is your real work.

The Eliventh Plague

I should warn you, this dream has cartoon DNA:
instead of sand, flags of pink confetti
undulate toward a roiling sea.

It's clear, I have escaped the sobriety of day.
I am drunk on nocturnal spirits
and see no reason to wean.

Living in the Kalamazoo of consciousness,
I am no longer beholden to the doctrine
of stripe, windows that auger transparency

or the correction of gravity.
On the pink, our roadster jumped ten feet,
and my pulse's pace leaped from near-stasis

to alarm. The driver, unknown and intimate
as dream personnel often are, mute, as they
often are, shrugged—what did I expect?

The confetti is fecund:
I glimpse it at dusk, exceeding its hours.
I glimpse it at lunch, voluble

with lubricious Rye grass and my blank-faced
driver takes a seat on a bench a discrete
distance away. His feet are blue

as sapphire. In a book of commentary
third cousin from the canon,
rebbes tell of the 11th plague: dream.

For one week, Egyptians could not separate
the visionary image from the real, adumbration
from memory, wish from remorse.

And Pharoah, in sleep-deprived stupor, said:
go stay go stay go
until God donned His pillar-of-cloud garb

and the Sea of Reeds rent to reveal
its fluxing floor. They left before
the 12th plague, metaphor, which the priests

glimpsed in spilled pile of grain that refused
to hold flame, and though famed
for deific beasts, they implored their ruler:

save us, save us from comparison, don't let
their God, the Unknown and Intimate,
reduce us to analogue, to figure, the limbo

of symbol, don't let Him
strike us down to
vehicle.

Three Fifty-Five A.M.

In the bossa nova of dream,
a collection of hips recollects
Antonio Carlos Jobim,
a dead dahlia redeems its bloom
in my fist and I realize it's going
to be harder to forget you
than I had hoped. You are like debt.
My doctor prescribed the beguine
and under his tutelage I
dutifully maneuvered until
I could forecast the weather in
Martinique by the pressure of
his palm on my back's concavity,
the way we spun. Still, you linger
beyond the notes suborned to song,
steady as a pinstripe in search
of a deep cuff and I can't help
listening while night's knees buckle
and the clock's face, persuaded, sways.

Four-Oh-Four A.M.

Same old ingredients: fan, shadow, furnishings.
How can I make a rich ragout from that?
Granted, the fan's revolutions
are nonviolent; the shadow has accordian pleats.

I am furnishing my dreams with lost
desires, found
objet d'merci,
having reread *La Belle Dame Sans Merci.*
I've renewed my membership
in the lost souls club.
The dues are low, the benefits few:
for thrall you get pallor
and an absence of birds

that sing—they will not bear witness
to night's provocations:
the insinuating cold
and the moon, a chaise longue for orphaned stars.

You should see the clerestory windows
our architect dreamed up:
a triptych of darkness other than our own.
Still, this is no Falling Water.
We are estranged from our environs—
as we intended. Intention should be
packed in your carry-on,
in case they lose your baggage

en route to waking. Can that be arranged—
a dream-scoured conscience?
What would propel, compel me through the day
if not the unsaid, undone?

Four Forty-Four A.M.

Please take away the mascotry of dream—
        those advocates of the illicit.
I am tired of old beaus who show up begging for gestures
        they never used to want.
Non-sequitors in lock-step
and then Father Coughlin shows up in drag
        smearing the Church of the Holy Flower
          with deficits of hate.
Looking like Hedy Lamaar, my mother
sighs. Would you like some tea
        with your Bleistein, Tom?

Dredge the bay of childhood for the silt and mud of memory:
        make a high-priced island, attracting exotics.
Surely those slim caws echo in the next world:
their voices claw at the sides of the cerebellum,
        slippery as a glass slipper, which leaves
        no treads. It is the perfect shoe
for committing a crime.
Why must death rhyme?
Little Bo Peep's crook swirled in blood like a maypole
        suspended from the basement of my youth,
and I woke up screaming.

Where was the ladybug, anyway?
While we were all on fire.

The brocade of symbols tattooed around my wrists and ankles
        cripples me gently.
Schooled, my knuckles rapped, I look for messages:
Dilarang merokok di kamar kecil: No smoking in lavatory.
83 for baby! 83 for baby! pants the asthmatic next-door.
I am not the lord's spinning wheel compleate,
        but wholly fractured, cubist to the bone.
We didn't need art to teach us
the cruelty of perspective: something and someone
                is always more important.
On that note: my daughter, screaming.

Four Fifty-Six A.M.

Such crying:
the tears flee their grot,
and find refuge in the nearest well
where townfolk, far from naïve,
drink, cook and wash with them
later to complain of feeling
forlorn for days—these tears
with no analogue in speech,
tasting like ovals,
wet as volition,
their provenance that of pleading,
though etymology, the bastard cousin of philology,
says "tears" and "tars" have more in common
than "tears" and "tiers"
or "tears" and "tires."
They are tired of being called sentimental.
"We are tired," they say.
How young we know salt's flavor—
when light unscrolls
its first folio.

Five Ten A.M.

The subconscious is orange and particular:
Phil what are you doing here?
what to make of
I never knew I wanted to make out
      a bass clef and jewel on the bed-frame?
      with Mike my daughter says
      A Jew in the bed, animate?
      the cow says Mike not moo
      A mirror outlined in mother-of-pearl
            my teeth are falling out I know
            buttons while the baby dozes, legs splayed
            that's normal
            with the grace found only when decorum
            I'm wearing no pants forgot my lines
            is sent to bed, supperless?
            and I know   *that's normal*
Hell if I know.   Must I spell it out?

Dragonfly, butterfly, ladybug—these are diminutive
      I was a detective investigating
      creatures, lapidary on the crib,
      the disappearance of Little Bo Peep
      bells in their bellies and wings.
and as I walked down the basement stairs
The latter's at the bar deep in flirtation
      saw her crook bloodied hanging
      while the house climbs in flame.
from the ceiling and I started to wail
So many opportunities for failure.
I had a flare for the histrionic
The view from here (the belvedere) is terrible:
is there still a hand   *beneath my bed*
please, don't tell me   how it all turns out.

If I were you I'd watch my back.
I learned to wake myself up

Five Thirty-One A.M.

Sleep leers in its full-sleeve tattoo
and dream refuses
to strike one of the forty prescribed poses
—harbinger of each year of your life—
you can hear the minions snickering
in the hinterlands.

You cannot even conscript
the light, high-wattage sconces
that bracket the bed in its baroque dress—
they would alert the others
that one of their company,
highly ranked,

won't glean a field for magic
beans once flung,
won't build a simple house
of straw of sticks of brick and boil
the enemy, reduce him
to stock—even if it means

the wolf recurs for weeks:
culpable vaguely, vaguely chosen
to represent all we can't control.
You stole those characters
from safe pages, after all, to serve
your personal dangers.

Drain the vials, lick the viands
of boredom. There is no nothingness
like the one that seeks you out.
The ropes that chafe day's wrists
are loosening. Soon it will
spit out the gag.

Three Friends

i. Interpret This

Butler and baker, both dreamed:
one of the vine, one of bread.
One filled up the Pharoah's cup.
One whose crumbs the birds devoured.
You will be restored, I told
the man whose night sang of wine.
The other hanged. The birds supped.

I told the Pharoah: *only*
God interprets dreams. I hope
you're on good terms, he winked. *Fat*
kine and full corn mean plenty.
Withered ears, of having none:
famine. Boom, bust. No one blinked.
Once, I dreamed I was the sun.

ii. The Butler's Quandary

Pity the baker his head
now separate from his torso
and served up *tartar* to birds,
hanged from the terebinth tree.
If I seem hard, it's that I
wonder: does dream instruct fate,
or from fate take its cruel cues?

And pity poor Joseph, stuck
in jail for being too good-
looking. I forgot about
him, the good turn he did me.
Now that Pharoah's dreams of kine
and corn keep us up at night,
should I let Joe save the day?

iii. The Baker's Lament

My specialty was angel
food cake: harder than it looks.
Inside each, I baked a small
angel: difficult to find,
unless you know their grottos
and habits. They like to scratch
the noses off our idols.

Of course, my source was bound to
dry up—and so, my pastries.
Jailed, I met a guy who sifts
signs and symbols. I told him
of the seven loaves atop
my head and saw his fallen
face. *Aw, say it ain't so, Joe.*

The Dreams Are One

Kings offend so easily.
The butler and baker in bad shape: *whadidIdo? whadidIdo?*
One pilfered change from Pharoah's Zoot suits, the other baked cakes
        shaped like the boss's daughter's breasts.
And they dreamed a dream, both of them, both bound for, bound in
prison—*interpretations belong to God*
said Joseph, *but I'll try for you, mon semblable, mon frère.*

And he said to the butler: *three days*
and you will be restored to office. Please, don't
forget me. Don't
let me rot down here in this dungeon where
all I have is dream: my little brother must be riding a trike by now
and reciting the Pledge of Allegiance with his hand pasted on his heart.
My brothers number eleven. My father longs for the twelfth.

And he said to the baker: *three days*
and Pharoah will divide your head from your body,
hang the latter from a tree like so—
and invite the birds to feast, sinew and limb. I am so
sorry—no, I don't understand God's feckless
nature. No, I—hey,
don't blame the messenger.

And the dreams of three
came—as Joseph read them—true. And Pharoah
dreamed of kine, seven lean devouring seven fat
and awoke in a sweat. And Pharoah
dreamed of corn, seven thin ears
devoured by seven full, and he awoke
in a sweat.

Then and only then
did the baker think of Joseph, who said: *interpretations belong*
to God but for you, mon capitaine, I'll try:
the seven good kine and the seven good ears
are years of plenty. The seven lean and thin, years of blight.
Do you see? The dreams are one.
Abundance, then famine: make your plans.

> *And since the dream was doubled,*
it will be done
by the God who speaks in twos—praised be He—
of three branches and baskets,
seven kine and ears of corn
and eleven brothers, plus one
who hums, *Summertime, and the livin' is easy,* who numbers
his dreams until he dies.

IV.

From the moment I picked up your book until I laid it down, I was convulsed with laughter. Some day I intend reading it.

—Groucho Marx

The Emergence of Hilarity, Chapter One

Once Upon a Time, when time was a series of scratched lines and gouged holes in sticks and bones, designed to evaluate the moon's phases, before time became an obelisk, a sundial, an hourglass, a pendulum, when the earth was innumerable and immeasurable, no one laughed. There was little to laugh about: preyed upon and preying upon the slower, the dumber, and the overwhelming sense of no control while the elements flailed in the chaos—this was not a world deserving of nostalgia like pre-war anywhere with its cafés of curved metal chairs that made anyone look more nuanced than average—this world was serious, its gravity psychic and physical—

The Emergence of Hilarity, Chapter Two

until one day one man named for the more tedious and remarkable stage of development, give or take a few hundred centuries, when he'd managed to kill a horned, furred deer and foolishly ran back to his shelter to tell the missus and then could not find his way back to said "deer" (not a deer, at all, the progenitor of some more feral creature that did not survive evolutionary peril, the entire population vanquished by one bad winter when a winter lasted the duration of a generation) chose to find the situation, if you can believe it, amusing rather than dire. For now, in lieu of the promised bounty, all he could offer was a befuddled apology, and that night and several after he would get only a stinky skin to warm his filthy feet. For some reason, he found this "funny": this was an exceptional guy, who centuries before would have stomped around the plains until he died of thirst or was killed by the family of the very animal he slaughtered, in a simplistic ambush.

The Emergence of Hilarity, Chapter Three

Not our hero. He found himself trying to explain while his mate, no wilting flower, began to wonder how he would taste, boiled with indigent herbs and roots. He gestured toward the entry of their dwelling as if to say, *hey, it's a big world out there and I swear I made the kill, you should have seen it, honey, we could have fed an army* except that they were loners, tribeless nomads who did not yet fathom the benefits of groups. As the tale grew, so did his gestures, the performance became acrobatic and when he reached the part about the creature which would be tougher than a cross between oysters and jerky, it happened: a staccato jolt, a gutteral flutter traveled from stomach to throat to mouth, reverberating in his fingers and once in the air, bounced off the walls haphazardly, either echoing or dully absorbed by their cave or hut, hut or cave.

The Emergence of Hilarity, Chapter Four

He heard it, she heard it. He could not stop, for it felt, it felt, it felt *good*, which he could only later describe as a feeling absent hunger, exhaustion and fear. At some point, his mate, certain that Whatever controlled avalanches and winged furies had captured Whatever within him made him open his eyes and rise with the light, and the only solution was to beat it out, beat it out, and so she did, with the large stick that leaned against their entranceway, where one day an umbrella with a curved handle would lounge. She aimed at his feet and hands, as they knew that ports of entry for what could only be called "evil" would be the extremities. Seeing this did no good except to make our hero dance to avoid her thrusts, she landed one squarely on his head and he slumped to the ground. This would be the end of the story—

The Emergence of Hilarity, Chapter Five

if irony were all, and the emergence of hilarity would be delayed until another age, and more generations of humorless *homo erectus* would wander the earth with little comfort, only occasionally wondering, *is that all there is?* Instead, our happy hunter recovered and succeeded in convincing his soulmate that his reaction was worthy of praise and repetition, since events such as the disappearing deer occurred often, and the usual vituperative fist-shaking did not, as he noted, bring back the deer. He would return many times to the clearing he believed the source of his mirth (he had taken the wrong turn at the forked tree) and established an altar there, of sorts, where he tested another practice, and began to think, to speak, to praise Whatever gave him the impulse to look beyond his loss and brought him back from the hard blows lovingly dealt. And the Divine Comedian who fashioned manwomandeershelter, out of a substance akin to vinegar dough (recipe to follow), agreed, this was a fine gift and should not be delayed, the time was right—people needed something to mitigate innumerable hardships, ordeals, obstacles, bad trips, and so around fourteen weeks (seven days took creation), when sound is voice is the absence of blood's loud tides, the child, prodded by the immeasurable, erupts, and the social smile begets a sort of music eliding joy and pain,

The Emergence of Hilarity, Chapter Seven

eliding joy and pain.

And it pleases all who hear.

Notes

"Where Were You, Nymphs?": Nereids are sea nymphs, dryads are wood nymphs, and oreads are mountain and hill nymphs.

"To Hope Street.": Dante was the man who layered hell like a taco salad.

"Porcine Dilemmas": the phrase *entre chien et loup* means "between dog and wolf" and refers to dusk or twilight.

"Pop Quiz:" the quotation, "Down, down, down—would the fall never come to an end?" is from Lewis Carroll's *Alice's Adventures Under Ground*.

B'rachot is Hebrew for blessings. It has a feminine ending. After Rilke; for Sydney.

"Instructions for the Good Life": the dream quotations are from *The Book of Legends*, edited by Hayim Nahman Bialik and Yehoshua Hana Ravnitzky.

"In re:" Epigraph, "Duck! God!": Jack McKasson, ten years old, attends Mariners Elementary.

"Your Name in the Title": Dybbuks are wandering souls believed in Jewish folklore to enter and possess a person.

"Break, Break, Break": title comes from a poem by Tennyson of the same name.

"Psalm to Night": "There are three keys which the Holy One, blessed be He, entrusts to no creature. . . but are kept in His own hand: the key of rain . . . the key of resurrection . . . and the key of the womb." *Pesikta Rabbati* 42:7.

"Still Life on Holiday with Nightmare": there are many wells in the Hebrew bible, including the one at which Rebecca met Isaac's manservant, who knew from her gesture that she was destined to be Isaac's wife.

"The Eleventh Plague": In Exodus 24, when Moses, Aaron, Nadab, Abihu and seventy elders behold God, there was "under His feet the like of a paved work of sapphire stone . . ."

"Four Forty-Four A.M.": Bleisten is a character in T.S. Eliot's poem, "Burbank with a Baedeker: Bleistein with a Cigar." Part of one line is borrowed from Edward Taylor: "Make me, O Lord, thy spinning wheel compleate . . ."

"The Dreams are One," "Interpret This," "The Baker's Lament," and "The Butler's Quandary" are based on the biblical story of Joseph, whose ascent to power hinged on his God-given ability to interpret the dreams of the baker and butler in jail with him, as well as those of the Pharoah.

Acknowledgements

ACM (Another Chicago Magazine): "3:55 A.M."

American Literary Review: "Psalm to Night"

The Antioch Review: "2:19 A.M."

Arbutus.net: "To Hope Street."

Askew: "4:04 A.M." and "4:44 A.M."

Barrow Street: "Anatomy of Disorder"

Image: "Ocean" and "Sand" from "In re:"

The Paris Review: "Where were you, Nymphs?"

Poetry: "What I Disliked About the Pleistocene Era" and "When I'm not feeling so good"

POOL: "1:21 A.M." and "3:39 A.M."

RHINO: "Pop Quiz: The Spider, Itsy Bitsy"

The Tampa Review: "Insomnia Manual"

Zeek.com: "B'rachot," "First Bookshelf," "The Alphabetizer Speaks," and "What I Disliked About the Pleistocene Era" appeared in the *Legitimate Dangers: American Poets of the New Century* (Sarabande Books, 2005) (Anthology).

"Sand" appeared in *Poetry Daily Essentials 2007*, eds. Diane Boller and Don Selby.

photo by Belle Amie Studios

Patty Seyburn's third book of poems, *Hilarity*, won the Green Rose Prize given by New Issues Poetry & Prose. She has published two books of poems: *Mechanical Cluster* (Ohio State University Press, 2002) and *Diasporadic* (Helicon Nine Editions, 1998) which won the 1997 Marianne Moore Poetry Prize and the American Library Association's Notable Book Award for 2000. Her poems have appeared in numerous journals including *The Paris Review, New England Review, Field, Slate, Crazyhorse, Cutbank, Quarterly West, Bellingham Review, Connecticut Review, Cimarron Review, Third Coast* and *Western Humanities Review.* Seyburn grew up in Detroit, earned a BS and an MS in Journalism from Northwestern University, an MFA in Poetry from University of California, Irvine, and a Ph.D. in Poetry and Literature from the University of Houston. She is an Assistant Professor at California State University, Long Beach and co-editor of *POOL*: A Journal of Poetry, based in Los Angeles. She lives with her husband, Eric Little, and their two children, Sydney and Will.

New Issues Poetry

David Dodd Lee, *Abrupt Rural; Downsides of Fish Culture*
M.L. Liebler, *The Moon a Box*
Alexander Long, *Vigil*
Deanne Lundin, *The Ginseng Hunter's Notebook*
Barbara Maloutas, *In a Combination of Practices*
Joy Manesiotis, *They Sing to Her Bones*
Sarah Mangold, *Household Mechanics*
Gail Martin, *The Hourglass Heart*
Justin Marks, *A Million in Prizes*
David Marlatt, *A Hog Slaughtering Woman*
Louise Mathias, *Lark Apprentice*
Gretchen Mattox, *Buddha Box, Goodnight Architecture*
Carrie McGath, *Small Murders*
Paula McLain, *Less of Her; Stumble, Gorgeous*
Lydia Melvin, *South of Here*
Sarah Messer, *Bandit Letters*
Wayne Miller, *Only the Senses Sleep*
Malena Mörling, *Ocean Avenue*
Julie Moulds, *The Woman with a Cubed Head*
Carsten René Nielsen, *The World Cut Out with Crooked Scissors*
Marsha de la O, *Black Hope*
C. Mikal Oness, *Water Becomes Bone*
Bradley Paul, *The Obvious*
Jennifer Perrine, *The Body Is No Machine*
Katie Peterson, *This One Tree*
Jon Pineda, *The Translator's Diary*
Donald Platt, *Dirt Angels*
Elizabeth Powell, *The Republic of Self*
Margaret Rabb, *Granite Dives*
Rebecca Reynolds, *Daughter of the Hangnail; The Bovine Two-Step*
Martha Rhodes, *Perfect Disappearance*
Beth Roberts, *Brief Moral History in Blue*
John Rybicki, *Traveling at High Speeds* (expanded second edition)
Mary Ann Samyn, *Inside the Yellow Dress; Purr*
Ever Saskya, *The Porch is a Journey Different from the House*
Mark Scott, *Tactile Values*
Hugh Seidman, *Somebody Stand Up and Sing*
Heather Sellers, *The Boys I Borrow*
Martha Serpas, *Côte Blanche*
Diane Seuss-Brakeman, *It Blows You Hollow*
Elaine Sexton, *Sleuth; Causeway*
Patty Seyburn, *Hilarity*
Marc Sheehan, *Greatest Hits*
Heidi Lynn Staples, *Guess Can Gallop*